THE UNOFFICIAL

PEDRO PASCAL

COLORING BOOK

We hope you enjoy this labor of love! Each design was lovingly hand rendered from a place of admiration. We'd really appreciate if you took the time to tell us what you think on amazon, and would be thrilled to see what you create with this book! Please enjoy this pocket of joy!

Daddy is a state of mind

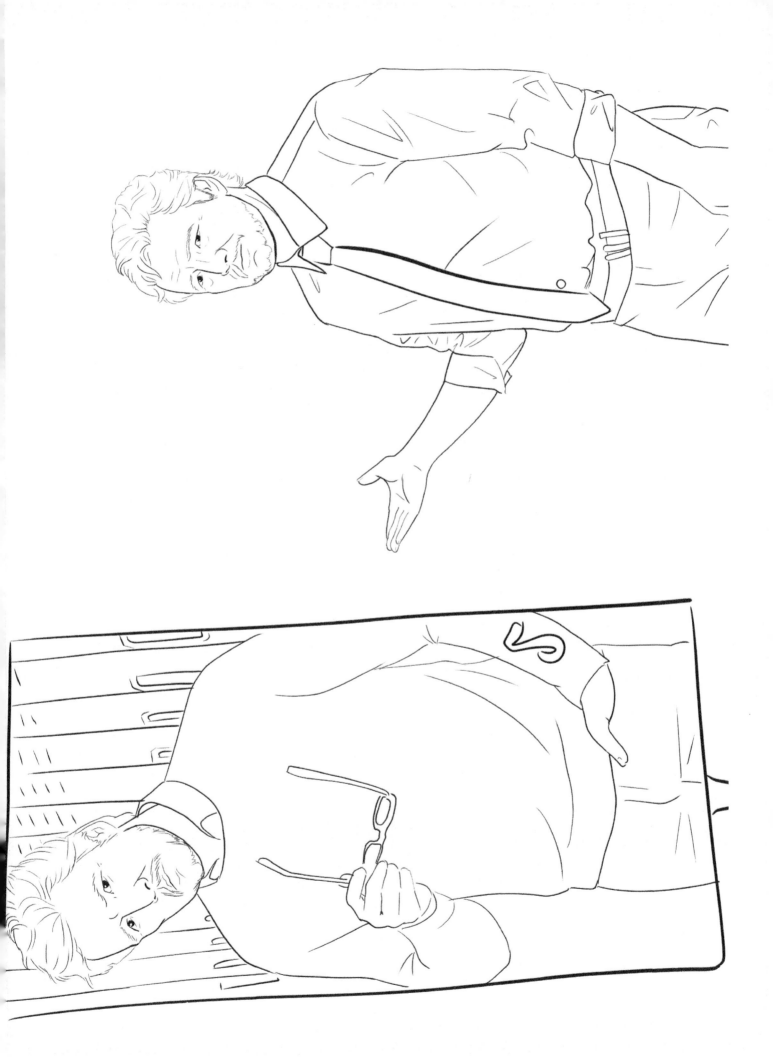

Don't make fancams of
school staff

I'm just going to sit here and say i love you and say hi and slay and yass

How would you like to ride home on a real cowboy?

DON'T DO DRUGS

—

WITHOUT ME

This is the way

No, that's how you spook a bear

Stop touching
things

it's okay, babygirl

I'm your cool, slutty daddy

VERY SHORT, BUT RAGGED BEARD

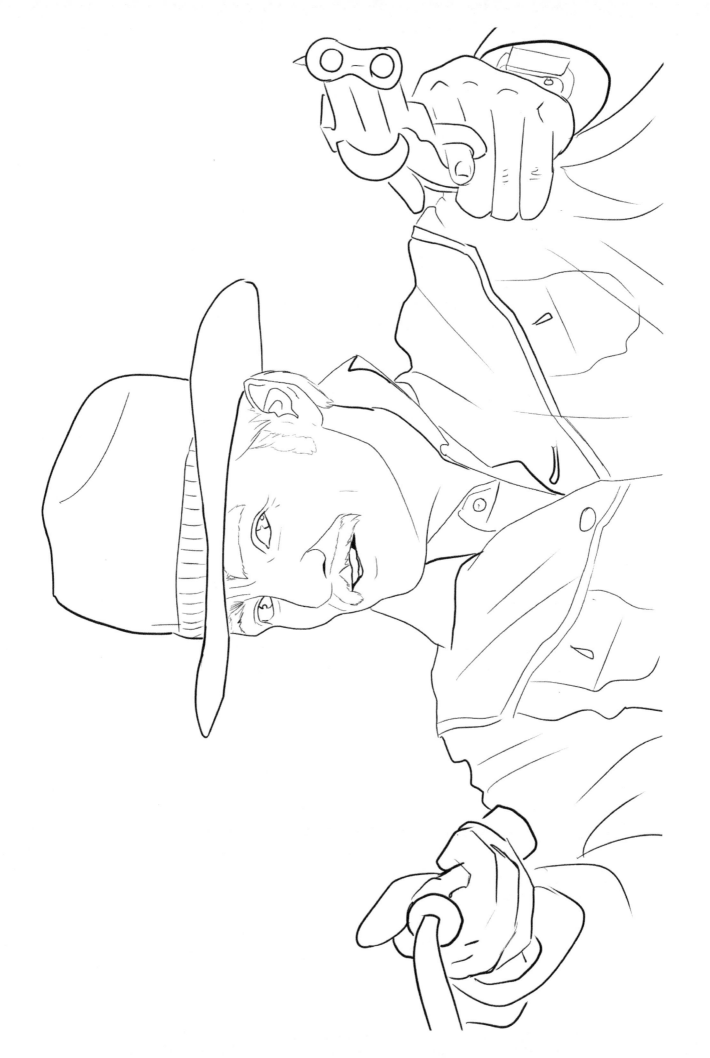

Pew - I'm running things

I go to every movie alone

Let's put a pin in that

He just like to jump

Let's call that one "Olivier"

A 706 page book about death

My most important
relationship - my ipad

papichulo

Daddy is a state of mind

WHY DID THE MONKEY FALL OUT OF THE
TREE?
'CAUSE IT'S DEAD.

I'm trying to care but it's hard

somebodygimmeahug

it's okay, babygirl

space daddy

when it's dark,

watch out

Daddy is a state of mind

I'm your cool, slutty daddy

I'm just going to sit here and say i love you and say hi and slay and yass

Manners
maketh
man

papichulo

Daddy is a state of mind

I DON'T NEED A HELMET

APRIL 2023

Printed in Great Britain
by Amazon

41597199R00040